ENGLISH LANGUAGE: PAPER TWO

An AQA Study Guide

ANTHONY WALKER COOK

First published in 2021 by Accolade Tuition Ltd
71-75 Shelton Street
Covent Garden
London WC2H 9JQ
www.accoladetuition.com
info@accoladetuition.com

Pages 38-39: Ka Bradley's 'Dancing virtually into the London Film Festival' (27/10/2020) was reproduced courtesy of *Springback Magazine*. Source: https://springbackmagazine.com/read/bfi-lff-expanded-dance-virtual-reality-documentary/. Many thanks to both Ka Bradley and Sanjoy Roy (editor at *Springback Magazine*).

Image, Page 17 ('Stay Home Save Lives') Copyright © Nina West. Licensed under CC BY-ND 2.0: https://creativecommons.org/licenses/by-nd/2.0/legalcode. Source: https://www.flickr.com/photos/nicasaurusrex/49863657318/

Image, Page 45 ('Virtual Reality Demonstrations') Copyright © Knight Center for Journalism in the Americas, University of Texas at Austin. Licensed under CC BY 2.0: https://creativecommons.org/licenses/by/2.0/legalcode.
Source: https://www.flickr.com/photos/utknightcenter/17191398541

Image, Page 48 ('newspaper') Copyright © VV Nincic. Licensed under CC BY 2.0.
Source: https://www.flickr.com/photos/blok70/32030163840

Image, Page 50 ('Lewisham University Hospital') Copyright © Reading Tom. Licensed under CC BY 2.0.
Source: https://www.flickr.com/photos/16801915@N06/9178132210

ISBN 978-1-913988-12-8

FIRST EDITION
1 3 5 7 9 10 8 6 4 2

Contents

Acknowledgments

I'd like to take a brief moment to thank a few people. Richard Davis at Accolade Press first approached me early last year to write a guide. Given this is now my third, you can say it has been a productive working relationship. My thanks to Richard come especially with the publication of this guide, which posed several issues regarding the sourcing of material.

I would also like to thank Ka Bradley and the editors of *Springback Magazine* for their permission to use the article 'Dancing Virtually into the London Film Festival', which was first published on October 27, 2020.

My partner, Carolina, has been a sounding board of teaching ideas over the past years. Herself a brilliant teacher, she continues to teach me many things.

My parents, Angela and Gordon, always emphasised the importance of education — to them, my thanks never seem enough.

Finally, I'd like to dedicate this guide to my students. From GCSE English Language to first-year university seminars, teaching remains one of my biggest passions. The resilience of all students the past year has been astounding. To those whom I have had the pleasure of knowing, thank you.

Some Notes on the Guide

A note on structure: Presented in this guide are four worked exams. In the first set of responses, I discuss the Assessment Objectives and consolidate your knowledge of what is expected for each question. In the second set, I outline my tips and tricks for each style of question. In the third set I suggest why some students struggle in their answers to the questions based on Examiner's Reports. Finally, the fourth set presents model answers with no introduction or commentary – they are for you to annotate and to explore the ways in which all of the questions for this exam can be answered.

A note on the chosen extracts: For this exam you will receive one text from the nineteenth century and one from **either** the twentieth or twenty-first century. Which depends on the date of the extract in Paper One. Whilst this may feel slightly intimidating, I cannot overstate the importance of reading widely. Students that read tend to have a better comprehension and vocabulary and are often more imaginative. If you're not sure what sort of books you're into, go to a local bookshop and ask; they'll have something to interest you!

A note on my analysis: You might notice that throughout my answers in this guide sometimes I refer to 'the writer' and others I name the writer directly. Either is fine: in the heat of the exam you might forget the author's name. The main point is that you're leading with an awareness that literature is actively written.

Editor's Foreword

If you're enrolled on AQA's English Language GCSE, you will be taking on two separate papers: Paper One – which deals with fiction – and Paper Two – which deals with non-fiction. This book (as you might have guessed from its title!) is designed to guide you specifically through Paper Two.

Now, before anything else, it's important to briefly outline what Paper Two looks like. The paper is comprised of two sections. The first section looks somewhat similar to comprehension papers students will have been doing throughout secondary school. You will be given two extracts from pieces of non-fiction (one will be from the past 120 years or so, and the other from the nineteenth century), and you will face four questions that deal with these extracts. These four questions – while of course tailored to the extracts in question – *always* take the same format, and are *always* worth a total of 40 marks (4 marks for the first question; 8 marks for the second; 12 marks for the third; and 16 marks for the fourth).

The medieval poet, Geoffrey Chaucer, is sometimes referred to as the 'Father of the English Language.' Above: the Chaucerian equivalent of a selfie.

Then, once you've cleared that hurdle, you'll have the second section to contend with: the non-fiction *writing* section. You'll be asked to write a piece of non-fiction on a topic related to the ideas discussed in the two extracts – it might be a newspaper article, it might be a speech, it might be a letter (heck, it could be *any* kind of non-fiction) – and this task is worth a further 40 marks.

I fully appreciate that this may all sound complex and daunting, but don't despair – as you work through this guide, the very talented Anthony (the author!) will take you through things step by step and shine a light into Paper Two's every nook and cranny.

And yet, having said all that, it is important to emphasise that this guide is *not* merely designed to familiarise you with Paper Two's structure; after all, there are already other great guides out there that do just that. Rather, this guide – by proffering model answers, dissecting this exemplar material, and painstakingly delving into AQA's mark-schemes – will seek to demonstrate *how* to ensure you are covering all bases and picking up every available mark. For while it is true that the extracts are unseen and thus you can never prepare fully in advance, there are all sorts of tactics and techniques that you can memorise and master before you set foot in that exam hall. In fact, it's precisely because we felt that no other guide adequately grapples with these techniques – adequately spells out how best to approach the paper's assorted challenges – that we decided to put together this dedicated technique guide for this exam in the first place!

They've been doing GCSE exams for a while now!

In short, our hope is that this book, by demonstrating *how* to tackle Paper Two's challenges, will help you feel more confident in doing so yourself. I believe that it is also worth mentioning that for most of the questions you'll encounter in Paper Two (in fact *all* except for Question 1) there is no one answer the examiner is looking for. That is, while Anthony's work may represent "model" material, someone else's answers could be quite different and yet be just as effective at nabbing the marks (this is especially true of the writing task in the paper's latter half!). I won't pretend your exam is likely to be *fun* – my memory of the exams is pretty much the exact opposite. But still, this is one of the very few chances that you will get at GCSE level to actually be creative. And to my mind at least, that was always more enjoyable – if *enjoyable* is the right word – than simply demonstrating that I had memorised loads of facts.

R. P. Davis, 2021

Sample Paper One

A 1914 poster celebrating the opening of the Charing Cross, Euston & Hampstead railway extension.

Grand Spectacles: The Great Exhibition & The London Underground

SECTION A: READING

Source A: *This extract is from an article published in the Family Economist, a cheap monthly periodical (a newspaper published at regular intervals) that wanted to encourage self-improvement in the working classes of Victorian England. The piece is a contemporary account of the Great Exhibition, an international exhibition held between May and October 1851 at the newly-built Crystal Palace in Hyde Park, London.*

1   Since the days of the Reform Bill, no event has caused so much wonder and excitement throughout the length and breadth of the land we live in as the Great Exhibition. Everybody, it is said, talks about it, and everybody may read about it if he will, in all sorts of books, newspapers, and other periodicals; and if anyone does not know

5   all about the huge building, its length, breadth, and capability, the number of iron pillars, miles of sash-bar, and feet of glass used in its construction – if any one does not know all this and more concerning the Crystal Palace, as it has been called, it must be because he does not want to know. We believe, however, that there are but very few of this class; for from every part of the kingdom we hear of thousands and

10 tens of thousands who are making preparations for a visit to London, drawn thither by the desire to see for themselves the magnificent collection of what art and industry can produce in all quarters of the world. Except the going up of the Jews to the feast of the Passover at Jerusalem, and the mighty gatherings for the crusades, we know of no event in history which has united so many minds in one common object.

15 Great numbers have already seen the sight, and have returned home again with something to talk about for many a year to come. It was the first visit that the greater

part of them had ever paid to London, and to have seen the Exhibition as well is a privilege which, according to the use made of it, will prove a temporary gratification, or a lasting benefit. To see the Exhibition is one thing, but to see it as it ought to be
20 seen is another. We propose, therefore, to offer a few remarks, which may be of service to such of our readers as are interested in the subject.

The working-classes generally will have but a limited time for their visits to the building; and it would be well for them to arrange beforehand how this time may be made the most of. If but a few hours are to be lost in their finding out what to do, it is so
25 much taken from the means of instruction and improvement. The first business on arrival in London will, of course, be to secure a lodging for the night, and the next step will be to get to Hyde Park. The first feeling on entering the grand edifice will be one of unqualified surprise and satisfaction, amounting, in many cases, to enthusiasm; and if this be not tempered by a little sober reflection, the chances are that the
30 articles displayed will not be studied as they deserve, but they will be looked at only as so many curiosities.

The great arch which runs across the centre of the building, or, as it is called, the transept, divides it into two equal parts, and we would recommend those who have two days for their visit to devote a day to each part. Enter the first day at the south
35 door of the transept, then turn to the left, and you will find yourself in the western half of the building, which contains the British portions of the Exhibition. Here are the articles brought together from all parts of England, Ireland, and Scotland, from Canada and other parts of our American possessions, from Australia, and from the East Indies. At the farthest end, on your left, as your look towards the west, are agri-
40 cultural implements, and specimens of woven goods, that is of cotton and linen, stuffs and clothes, canvass and cambrie, silk and satin, in almost innumerable variety.

Source B: *This extract is from a sketch, 'Touring in the Tubes', in Arthur H. Bevan's Tube, Train, Tram and Car (1903). Written at a time when the tube was still an emerging experience, the sketch follows Mrs Rosamond on her morning journey on the tube to visit her aunt.*

---

1 The booking-office was full of people – of the working class, thought fair Mrs. Rosamond, who, observing that each person paid the sum of three-halfpence through the glass partition that screened the clerks from too close contact with the public, tendered that modest sum like the others, without specifying her destination. But
5 though plainly, she was too daintily dressed and too self-evidently a lady to escape notice, and was rather surprised at being asked if she wanted a workman's ticket. "Oh no!" she hastily exclaimed. "I am only going to the Bank, and then to Islington

on a visit." "Well, then, your fare is twopence." And she received in return a small slip of paper and not the familiar paste-board ticket covered with undecipherable
10   letters and figures.

Following the crowd, Mrs. Rosamond dropped the document into a sloping box fixed at the side of the gate and presided over by a railway official, the process suggesting to her lively imagination the method by which votes are recorded at a School Board election.

15   Wide open stood the door of a gigantic lift, the like of which she had never seen, which quickly filled with a compact mass of some fifty men and a sprinkling of women. There were upholstered benches at the sides; and a civil young artisan offered her his seat, but Lilian preferred to stand and look about her. The electro-lighted apartment was not aesthetic, and the unsightly advertisements, and notices
20   warning travellers against smoking, spitting, or standing too near the doors, did not add to its beauty; and when the telescopic gates were clashed together and fastened, the whole thing reminded Mrs. Rosamond of a great cage full of specimens of the British Homo Sapiens packed for conveyance and exhibition to inhabitants of other regions.

25   Suddenly, gently, and noiselessly the lift began to descend, and it seemed as if it would never stop. But stop it did, at a depth of seventy feet, which might have been seven hundred so far as Mrs. Rosamond's sensations were concerned. Once again the iron gates clashed, and the wild animals – I mean the passengers – streamed forth, our fair traveller following, to the platform.

30   Was she dreaming? Had she, like Alice in Wonderland, suddenly become diminutive, and was she waiting for a well-groomed little white rabbit, with gold watch and chain, to emerge from what resembled a burrow at the end of the station? It was so very small. Everything was on a reduced scale, the standing-room was a mere strip of planking, the tube like a pea-shooter. Surely it would not take in the train! However, it
35   was deliciously cool and light, and the tiles that lined the station were, as she found by touching them with her gloved hands, perfectly free from smuts.

In a few moments, from the open cutting at the opposite end of the platform, where lay the shunting tracks, a bright light and metallic clattering heralded the strange-looking chimneyless locomotive. Behind it came five attractive-looking cars joined
40   together, and gleaming with light. At their point of junction were telescopic gates, flung open as soon as the train stopped, and Mrs. Rosamond, who had just time to observe that there were not two rails only on the track, but a third in the middle, hurried into the first car she could find, and the earliest train on the Tube glided into the tunnel *en route** for the Bank.

* on the way to

Question One: Guidance

Questions One and Two are both marked by AO1, which is the ability to identify and interpret explicit and implicit information and ideas and to select and synthesize evidence from different texts. Question One assesses the first of these two points.

Question One is meant to ease you into the exam and will take the form of a multiple choice question. You will have to read the first few lines of the extract and will then be presented with eight statements. The task is to choose which four of them are true.

The statements will test your ability to draw both explicit (that which is plainly stated) and implicit (that which is implied) information from the chosen extract; they are not written to trick you, nor will they be deliberately ambiguous. You might, however, have a statement that is similar to a line in the extract, but that means something different. You can read about an example of where this happened in the November 2018 Examiner's Report. On the subject of Examiner's Reports, you should consult them for all your subjects: they can give you plenty of tips and tricks and they outline where students went wrong, which is an equally valuable lesson to learn. Remember, this question is about reading comprehension, so take your time.

Question One: Exemplar

Read again the first part of **Source A** from **lines 1 to 12.**

Choose four statements below which are **true.**

[4 marks]

1. The event has prompted excitement across the country.
2. Everybody has a free ticket to the event.
3. Reports about the Great Exhibition can be found in various publications.
4. The exhibition is housed in a small building.
5. The building is made of copper.
6. The Great Exhibition is being housed in the Crystal Palace.
7. People are planning on visiting the exhibition from across the country.
8. Transport links are being overwhelmed because so many are trying to get to London.

Question Two: Guidance

Question Two continues to assess AO1, but this time it is also looking at your ability to select and synthesize evidence from different texts.

The task is to identify either similarities, differences or details about a topic between the two texts and synthesize this material. By 'synthesize' I mean you have to bring various parts of the text together and form a new point. Remember how photosynthesis is the process plants use to turn light energy into chemical energy in the form of glucose (and you thought this was a revision guide just for English) – well, you need to adopt a similar process here: turn your reading and the details of the text (the sunlight) into inferences (the energy).

But what do I mean by the word 'inferences'? To infer means to form an opinion or assume that something is true based on the information you have. So, if someone is walking really quickly you might infer they're in a hurry; or if you see someone in a sling you might infer they've broken their arm. Lower grade students are those who can select and compare textual detail but who fail to make inferences from that information. It is in the detailing of the inferences that you gain marks: to get into the Level 3 band (5-6 marks out of 8) your observations have to be unarguable or unquestionable. To achieve this, you need to have a precise or detailed inference.

You will need to refer to **both** sources in this answer (if you only write about one text, you will achieve a maximum of 4 marks). This task will have a narrow focus, and as such when you're reading through the work it might not seem as if there is a ton of information to write about. This is where the process of inferring or making inferences comes into play. You should aim to present two or three comparisons with brief quotations (integrated quotations are always better than lengthy ones) or textual details.

Question Two: Exemplar

You need to refer to **Source A** and **Source B** for this question.

Both of these sources describe new buildings or spaces in London.

Write a summary of what you understand about the designs of these new buildings.

[8 marks]

*Whilst reading Source A, it is impossible not to be struck by the size of the **building: the writer describes 'the number of iron pillars, miles of sash-bar, and feet*** *of glass used in its construction'.[1] The focus on these materials conjures the image of a tall building that might even be difficult* **to fully define owing to the use of glass throughout the building. It is, after all, a 'Crystal Palace', and there is a distinct sense of the ingenuity of the building's design.[2]** *A similar indefinable quality is in Source B, but instead of focusing on height, the writer in Source B suggests how deep underground Mrs. Rosamond journeys. Although it goes down to* **'seventy feet',[3]** *Mrs Rosamond is so confused that it 'might have been seven hundred'. This is because the journey down effects her 'sensations'.* **Both texts,[4]** *then, in focusing on the size and scale of the buildings, emphasise the impressive scale of these new works that often had a dizzying effect on the imagination.*

*1) **Always keep your quotations as short as possible.** You probably don't ever want it much longer than what I've quoted here. 2) **An example of how I'm inferring about the design from the details in the text.** 3) **Notice how my quotation is here shorter and integrated into my own writing.** 4) **Note here how I'm drawing the two together to form a conclusion.** 5) **I'm here using parenthesis to show my comprehension of the text.** 6) **Notice how throughout this paragraph I'm adding details to support my comments and inferences.** 7) **Again I conclude with a summative point that brings both sources together.***

Yet the size of the Crystal Palace is not necessarily a good thing: **it (and the exhibition it holds)[5]** *is so large that it requires a period of orientation to understand. People can easily lose 'a few hours' 'in their finding out what to do'. As such it is* **necessary to plan the trip** *to the building so as to benefit as much as possible from what's inside: the large size of the building means that there is much potential of 'instruction and improvement' for* **a prepared viewer***. Against this* **prestige** *might be contrasted the* **dirty tube[6]** *that Mrs Rosamond visits. Against the show of the Crystal Palace there is a focus on utility on the tube: signs warn against spitting and smoking, the lights are 'not aesthetic' but sufficiently do the job, and the tiles are 'perfectly free from smuts'.* **Whilst the tube lacks the grandness and beauty of the Crystal Palace, then, it is perfectly suited to its purpose of helping Londoners get around.[7]**

Question Three: Guidance

Question Three assesses AO2, which is the ability to 'Explain, comment on and analyse how writers use **language** and **structure** to achieve effects and influence readers, using relevant subject terminology to support their views.' You should be familiar with the demands of AO2 from Paper One, where it is assessed in both Questions Two (commenting on language) and Three (commenting on structure).

The thing to remember for Question Three is that you need to talk about **effect**. Remember one thing when you're reading: someone sat down and wrote that text. Be it a great play like *Macbeth*, a grand Dickensian novel, a diary entry or a niche piece of travel writing, the author of that text decided on each metaphor, each piece of punctuation, each joke. The list goes on and on. AO2 assesses your ability to analyse these features. Over the years the exam has been running, the mean mark achieved by students for Question Three has held around the lower end of Level 2 (4-6 marks). This means the candidate shows some understanding of how language is used by a writer but they don't comment on effect. If you can conquer this skill, you'll be well on your way to doing well in both English Language and English Literature at GCSE level.

Question Three: Exemplar

You now need to refer only to Source B from **lines 11 to 29**.

How does the writer use language to describe Mrs Rosamond's experience at the station?

[12 marks]

1) My opening statement explains my argument throughout the response. Paragraphs are then grouped into themes. 2) Throughout my response, no technique is named without a comment on its effect. 3) Again quotations are integrated into my response. Focusing on the effect of an individual word is a valid way of analysing language. 4) If writing about sound effects (onomatopoeia, alliteration, etc) it's always good to draw attention directly to the word/sound you're analysing.

*Throughout the extract, the writer shows how Mrs Rosamond's experience at the station is **both scary and new.**[1] Mrs Rosamond is described as having a 'lively imagination', which is captured in the narrative's constant deflating of the unfamiliar journey she is about to take down to the tube. Before she has even entered the lift, Mrs Rosamond likens the way of putting her ticket into the box to the ways 'votes are recorded at a School Board election', with the **writer's use of analogy adding an almost comic tone to the extract.**[2]*

*Mrs Rosamond is then met with a 'gigantic lift' into which she enters with 'a compact mass of some fifty men and a sprinkling of women'. The word **'sprinkling'**[3] adds a lighter tone to these women and emphasises how few of them are in the lift. Not only, however, are the women surrounded by men, but they are also in a space that is politely described by Mrs Rosamond as 'not aesthetic'. The 'unsightly advertisements' and notices 'against smoking, spitting, or standing too near the doors' are both emphasised and connected through the writer's use of sibilance, creating a thoroughly unpleasant space. The writer also describes how the gates 'clashed together', with the **onomatopoeic*** *'**clashed**'*[4] *adding a harsher tone still to this space. Yet this is contrasted again with Mrs Rosamond's humorous observation that all these people, packed into the lift as they are, reminds her of a stuffy museum exhibition.* ***Although the writer wants to present Mrs Rosamond's experience as grimy and loud, then, the character is also established as a pleasant, joking figure amidst this grim and loud setting.***[5]

*5) **A summative comment to draw all my analysis together.** 6) **Brackets unobtrusively provide the evidence for my comment.** 7) **Again just a final comment to draw everything together.***

The writer uses a ***triplet of verbs ('Suddenly, gently, and noiselessly')***[6] *to establish the uncanny movement of the lift. This confuses Mrs. Rosamond, who is not sure how far down she goes. Yet in spite of this confusion, a final joking observation concludes the paragraph, for when the gates open it is described how 'the wild animals — I mean the passengers — streamed forth'. The writer's use of parenthesis to clarify the metaphor implies Mrs Rosamond's ironic outlook.* ***Her experience, then, is one of awe and fear; but these features are tempered by a warm, humorous narrative voice that presents this new technology as something not necessarily to be feared.***[7]

Question Four: Guidance

Question Four requires you to show evidence of AO3, meaning you have to be able to compare writers' ideas and perspectives on a certain topic. You might have to explore similarities or differences between the texts.

This is a much more open question: you need to engage with both sources **in their entirety.** That said, keep your answer focused on the topic of the question: in order to get into Level 3 (9-12 marks) of the mark scheme, your answers need to be 'clear' and 'relevant'.

However, one vital part of the question often confuses students: the focus on the 'methods' used to convey the topics outlined in the sources. What does 'methods' mean? Well, you can draw on the sort of language techniques (similes, metaphors, repetition, alliteration, etc) you will have been looking at in Question Three, but you might also want to think about the use of structure (as per Question Three in Paper One).

The fact is, 'methods' refers to any of the ways in which a writer conveys their ideas. If it's a little daunting, just remember that you have already used the skills needed for this task: you've synthesised and compared in Question Two and you've analysed methods in Question Three (although it should be noted that the focus of Questions Three and Four will always be different and, as such, you should not use the same material in both answers).

The list would go on and on if we were to outline every single feature. However, some things you might want to think about generally include:

• Tone – what is the tone of the work? By this I mean the way in which the writer approaches their topic. The tone can be all manner of things, but if you can understand it – is it ironic, angry, enthusiastic, sympathetic – then you'll really be able to get underneath the writer's intention.

• What sort of language is used? Is it humorous, emotional, angry? This feature is very much linked with tone.

• Who is telling the story, or what is their intent? We're going to cover this in more detail in the notes on Question Five, but each source has a specific audience and intent, and the writer will use certain methods to successfully get its message across. Be alert also to the fact that a person brings their own assumptions and beliefs to a piece of non-fiction, and they will use literary techniques to amplify these ideas and arguments. Identifying and writing about these methods is part of the skill for Question Four.

You will need to make sure you are strict with your timings throughout the first section of this exam. Otherwise, as has been noted in previous Examiner's Reports, you will not have enough time for Question Four. Remember, this is worth 16 marks, so you need to spend an adequate amount of time on it.

Question Four: Exemplar

For this question, you need to refer to the **whole of Source A**, together with the **whole of Source B**.

Compare how the writers convey their different feelings about these new spectacles.

In your answer, you could:

- compare their different attitudes
- compare the methods the writers use to convey their different attitudes
- support your response with references to both texts.

[16 marks]

1) *A simple opening sentence to make my point clearly.* 2) *Just as in Question Three, you've got to write about the effects of literary techniques (the 'methods' in the second bullet point).* 3) *Comparative language ensures I'm achieving AO3 marks.* 4) *My parenthesis adds detail and a little more analysis.* 5) *At the end of the paragraph I'm ensuring I compare the two sources.* 6) *You don't need to explain every reference, but it can be useful to acknowledge them.* 7) *Lots of literary techniques are discussed throughout this paragraph and always with a focus on their effect.* 8) *Again, comparative language.* 9) *Phrases like this ensure the examiner is aware I'm ranging throughout the source.*

The tone throughout Source A is one of celebration.[1] *The Great Exhibition offers an event that has 'united so many minds' — it transcends class boundaries and allows the working-classes to learn about both England and the empire. In the first paragraph,* **the writer uses hyperbole**[2] *in declaring 'we know of no event in history which has united so many minds in one common object' to focus on the scale of the event. This is also emphasised by the writer's use of comparisons, first to the Reform Bill of 1832 and then to the religious and historical events of Passover and the crusades respectively, which cast the Great Exhibition as an almost religious experience.* ***Compared to this***,[3] *however, might be the monotony of the other travellers throughout Source B. As delightful as Mrs Rosamond is* **(she is 'daintily dressed' with the alliteration adding a pleasing note to this description),**[4] *the frequent reference to animals throughout Source B dehumanises the travellers: in the lift Mrs Rosamond imagines herself with her other travellers as 'a great cage full of specimens'. Indeed the influence of the Great Exhibition, which is about display, could be seen to have influenced Mrs Rosamond's thinking, for the cage is to be displayed to the 'inhabitants of other regions'. For all Mrs Rosamond's interest, then, she stands out amidst a darker world.* ***The tube is, by comparison to the Great Exhibition, a dark place.***[5]

However with this darkness the author of Source B does find imaginative potential. Once Mrs Rosamond has travelled down to the train level, she asks 'Was she dreaming?' The world below ground is small, with the **reference**[6] *to 'Alice in Wonderland' adding a fairy-tale quality to the story. Mrs Rosamond's attempts to understand this new world is captured by the* **writer's use of questions.** *Looking around her, Mrs Rosamond cannot believe the train will be able to fit through the small tunnel ahead of her. The writer's* **simile 'like a pea-shooter' emphasises**[7] *the narrowness of the tunnel: everything in this underground space is out of proportion and difficult to believe. The Great Exhibition* **likewise necessitated a suspension of belief, but for different reasons.**[8] *Its size and scope, according to the writer, means that 'a little sober reflection' is needed for its full effect to be recognised and achieved. The word 'sober' implies that other visitors are intoxicated with the opportunities presented by the Exhibition. Instead, the 'many curiosities' must be enjoyed with a clear mind, through which the exhibition is almost cast as a treasure of endless possibilities.*

Towards the end of Source A,[9] *the writer uses lists to capture the 'almost innumerable variety' of what might be seen at the Exhibition. These words all defy singular definition, and thus celebrate the unknown grandeur of the Exhibition.* ***Likewise*** *Source B offers some solace: whilst the*

10) *Really honing in on a particular part of the text to add detail to my answer.*
11) *A final sentence just to tie everything together.*

dimensions of the tunnels are unusual, when the train arrives it is 'heralded' by bright lights, implying its grand status. The train is 'gleaming with light' and made up of 'attractive-looking cars', and the writer uses interjections to suggest Mrs Rosamond's wonder: **she 'had just time' to learn about the train tracks**[10] before stepping on. At the end of the passage, it is noted how the train 'glided' off towards the next stop, with the word suggesting Mrs Rosamond's journey was to be smooth and pleasant. **Both Sources A and B, therefore, offer visions of a new world of gleaming technologies.**[11]

An illustration of the 1851 Great Exhibition at the Crystal Palace.

There's nothing better than leaving home?

SECTION B: WRITING

Question Five: Guidance

Just when you thought you was coming to the end of your exam, you're hit with the fifth and final question – and it's a whopper. Whereas Section A has you explore the viewpoints of others on a certain topic, Section B lets you have your own say on this same topic. You'll often be given a controversial point and you'll be invited to respond to it. Based on previous examination papers, you'll likely have to say whether or not you agree or disagree with this controversial opinion – although there's also a chance that you might just have to explain your view on something instead of coming down on a particular side.

The marks for Question Five are split into two: AO5 (Content and Organisation) and AO6 (Technical Accuracy). Don't worry, we haven't missed AO4: that is only assessed in Paper One!

The terms of AO5 can be split and independently defined: 'Content' refers to: your register (that is, the tone and vocabulary you use to grab your audience); the way in which your piece is matched to its purpose (hence those little pre-ambles); and the ideas and techniques you employ in your creative writing piece. 'Organisation' meanwhile refers to your use of structure alongside ideas that are, for top marks, compelling and convincing.

AO6 is what we might reductively call Spelling, Punctuation and Grammar (SPaG), but at the top of the mark scheme it is about both accuracy and using a range of sentence structures and ambitious vocabulary. To access the top end of the scheme, there also needs to be a range of punctuation used (ideally including brackets, colons and semi-colons).

Question Five: Exemplar

'Whether it be travelling abroad or a staycation, there's nothing better than leaving home and trying something new.'

Write a newspaper article in which you argue your point of view in response to this statement.

(**24 marks for content and organisation**
16 marks for technical accuracy)
[40 marks]

OUT WITH THE NEW AND IN WITH THE OLD

Staying in, according to Anthony Walker-Cook, is the new thing to do.[2]

When the world was put on pause due to the coronavirus, households across the country began enjoying working from home. No longer did the **weary**[3] office worker have to leave home at 5am; they also avoided having to stand in a train of commuters packed in like sardines. The hours spent daily on the M25 were transformed into lie ins. DIY projects came to life as weekends at home became an opportunity to paint the third bedroom pink or re-grout the bathroom. **If the coronavirus has taught us anything, it's that staying at home can, in fact, be as fun as getting out.**[4]

Working 9 to 5[5]

Before the pandemic, we were living to work. Days, weeks and months were spent in the mindless trudge of everyday life where too much time was spent on things that did not matter. But now we've been presented with an opportunity to re-set our attitudes about work and home. Now, from the comfort of our couch, we can learn a new skill: **researchers at the University of Oxford found that at least 60% of the population attempted to learn something new during the first lockdown.**[6] Popular new hobbies have ranged

1) **Because this is a newspaper, you need a catchy title – spend time thinking about common phrases and idioms that could make for snappy one-liners.** 2) **My by-line explains the argument of the piece.** 3) **Well placed adjectives like 'weary' add flavour to my work.** 4) **I'm ending my first paragraph by providing my 'argument' – this way, the examiner knows exactly where I'm heading throughout my answer.** 5) **Subtitles neatly organise the work – here I'm using a well-known phrase to grab attention.**

from knitting to flower arranging, from boxing to stamp collecting. With YouTube and other streaming sites offering countless tutorials from an endless number of professionals, there's never been a better time to try something unusual.

6) Statistics should be used sparingly, but they can be useful to support your point (note also how I'm using a colon, showing higher-level punctuation).

Moreover, the way we approach work has changed. Numerous companies have noted how workers are more efficient within their working hours — **their only crime is that they raid the cookie jar too often**.[7] *But we must embrace this changing lifestyle and, in turn, adapt to it: it's time to think about investing in a desk-chair that supports your back or improve the lighting in your study. With internet shopping so advanced and efficient, making these changes has never been easier.*

A Recipe for Success[8]

At the beginning of the pandemic, you couldn't **scroll** *on social media without seeing a recently-baked sourdough loaf. Whilst supermarkets* **cried out** *for more bags of flour, the nation it seemed got creative and learnt how to cook better food. Where's the problem with that? As popular high-street cafes have slowly* **eroded** *our desire to make our own sandwiches, now we're willing to make everything from scratch. Over the past few years the various food-delivery apps have created a culture in which we don't think our own cooking is up to scratch with the restaurant's down the road. Now people don't* **wince**[9] *at the thought of cooking an extravagant meal.* **Words such as 'sear', 'flambé' and 'prove' have entered our vocabularies.**[10]

Alongside this,[11] *the impulse to 'get abroad' has been dampened. A 10 day holiday in the sun for a family of four traditionally cost anything between £750 and £3000. That money is now being put towards new laptops and other home improvements.* **Fresh licks of paint, newly-tiled bathrooms and house extensions are employing hundreds if not thousands of handymen who have received little financial support during the pandemic. In this way, we're pumping money back into local businesses.**[12]

7) Little moments of humour can really add to your piece. 8) My subtitle here is a play on the section's theme. 9) Notice throughout this paragraph how I've sprinkled in effective words. 10) Likewise, in writing this list, I'm showing off my own vocabulary. 11) Notice my use of accretive language throughout my answer ('Moreover', 'Alongside this') as a way of suggesting how I'm presenting multiple arguments. 12) This paragraph uses both long and short sentences for effect. 13) A semi-colon here shows my ability to use top-level punctuation.

Obviously, I'm not calling for an end to holidays or **restaurants; when**[13] *the time comes we must support these industries wholeheartedly. Of course we'll want to go out for dinner or travel to a*

new destination again, but surely it's better that we've all learnt the benefits of enjoying what we have instead of always wanting more?[14]

14) Rhetorical questions are a great way to get your examiner thinking in a way that will hopefully bring them around to your way of thinking. 15) A neat simile to give over the idea of adventure and excitement. 16) A clear final sentence that ties my argument together.

One thing that has certainly come from the pandemic is the stronger sense of community. Whereas before it was common not to know your neighbour, people now are reaching out. From baking a cake to a prolonged chat, it's vital that we get to know as many people as possible so that we can all support one another. We're also learning more about our local areas and the beauty that can there be found: long walks reveal secrets **as if**[15] the places we've been living in for years are long-lost kingdoms.

We've been conditioned over the past decades to believe that the lives we were living weren't sufficient. **But now living at home has provided us all with the opportunity to think again and to learn something new.**[16]

As a result of the outbreak of Covid-19, people across the UK were required to stay at home for much of 2020 — and beyond. Copyright © Nina Grant

Sample Paper Two

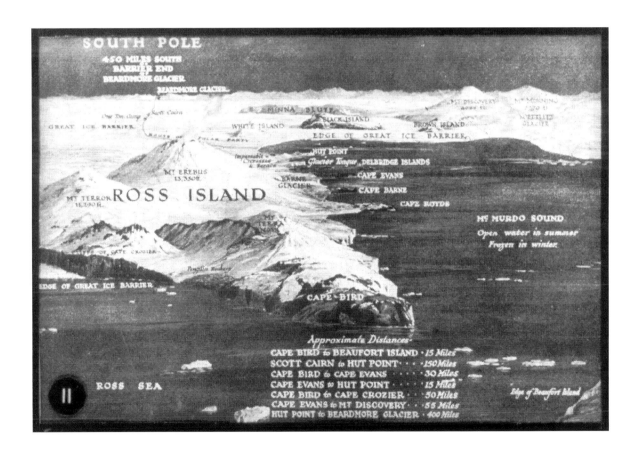

Extreme Conditions: Sierra Leone & A Storm at Sea

Source A: *Mary Henrietta Kingsley first arrived in Sierra Leone on 17 August, 1893. Travels in West Africa is Kingsley's own good-natured account of what she found on her second trip. In Source A, Kingsley records an afternoon in the forest, which includes a particularly violent storm.*

---

1   A little after two o'clock I return to camp, after having wandered about in the forest and found three very deep holes, down which I heaved rocks and in no case heard a splash. In one I did not hear the rocks strike, owing to the great depth. I hate holes, and especially do I hate these African ones, for I am frequently falling, more or less, 5   into them, and they will be my end.

The other demijohns* of water have not arrived yet, and we are getting anxious again because the men's food has not come up, and they have been so exceedingly thirsty that they have drunk most of the water - not, however, since it has been in Monrovia's charge; but at 3.15 another boy comes through the bush with another 10   demijohn of water. We receive him gladly, and ask him about the chop.** He knows nothing about it. At 3.45 another boy comes through the bush with another demi-john of water; we receive him kindly; *he* does not know anything about the chop. At 4.10 another boy comes through the bush with another demijohn of water, and knowing nothing about the chop, we are civil to him, and that's all.

15   A terrific tornado which has been lurking growling about then sits down in the forest and bursts, wrapping us up in a lively kind of fog, with its thunder, lightning, and rain. It was impossible to hear, or make one's self heard at the distance of even a few

paces, because of the shrill squeal of the wind, the roar of the thunder, and the rush of the rain on the trees round us. It was not like having a storm burst over you in the least; you felt you were in the middle of its engine-room when it had broken down badly. After half an hour or so the thunder seemed to lift itself off the ground, and the lightning came in sheets, instead of in great forks that flew like flights of spears among the forest trees. The thunder, however, had not settled things amicably with the mountain; it roared its rage at Mungo***, and Mungo answered back, quivering with a rage as great, under our feet. One feels here as if one were constantly dropping, unasked and unregarded, among painful and violent discussions between the elemental powers of the Universe. Mungo growls and swears in thunder at the sky, and sulks in white mist all the morning, and then the sky answers back, hurling down lightnings and rivers of water, with total disregard of Mungo's visitors. The way the water rushes down from the mountain wall through the watercourses in the jungle just above, and then at the edge of the forest spreads out into a sheet of water that is an inch deep, and that flies on past us in miniature cascades, trying the while to put out our fire and so on, is - quite interesting. (I exhausted my vocabulary on those boys yesterday.)

As soon as we saw what we were in for, we had thrown dry wood on to the fire, and it blazed just as the rain came down, so with our assistance it fought a good fight with its fellow elements, spitting and hissing like a wild cat. It could have managed the water fairly well, but the wind came, very nearly putting an end to it by carrying away its protecting bough house, which settled on "Professor" Kefalla, who burst out in a lecture on the foolishness of mountaineering and the quantity of devils in this region. Just in the midst of these joys another boy came through the bush with another demijohn of water. We did not receive him even civilly; I burst out laughing, and the boys went off in a roar, and we shouted at him, "Where them chop?" "He live for come," said the boy, and we then gave him a hearty welcome and a tot of rum, and an hour afterwards two more boys appear, one carrying a sack of rice and beef for the men, and the other a box for me from Herr Liebert, containing a luxurious supply of biscuits, candles, tinned meats, and a bottle of wine and one of beer.

* A demijohn is usually a large bottle that can contain 3 to 10 gallons of water.

** Chop refers to food or dinner.

*** The mountain Mungo Mah Lobeh.

Source B: *Source B is taken from Robert Falcon Scott's diary. Scott undertook an ill-fated journey to the Antarctic in June 1910 but he would not return. Another team of explorers found his body with his records and diaries in November 12, 1912.*

1 *Friday, December* 1.—A day of great disaster. From 4 o'clock last night the wind fresh-
ened with great rapidity, and very shortly we were under topsails, jib, and staysail
only. It blew very hard and the sea got up at once. Soon we were plunging heavily
and taking much water over the lee rail. Oates and Atkinson with intermittent
5 assistance from others were busy keeping the ponies on their legs. Cases of petrol,
forage, etc., began to break loose on the upper deck; the principal trouble was caused
by the loose coal-bags, which were bodily lifted by the seas and swung against the
lashed cases. 'You know how carefully everything had been lashed, but no lashings
could have withstood the onslaught of these coal sacks for long'; they acted like
10 battering rams. 'There was nothing for it but to grapple with the evil, and nearly all
hands were labouring for hours in the waist of the ship, heaving coal sacks overboard
and re-lashing the petrol cases, etc., in the best manner possible under such difficult
and dangerous circumstances. The seas were continually breaking over these people
and now and again they would be completely submerged. At such times they had to
15 cling for dear life to some fixture to prevent themselves being washed overboard, and
with coal bags and loose cases washing about, there was every risk of such hold being
torn away.'

'No sooner was some semblance of order restored than some exceptionally heavy
wave would tear away the lashing and the work had to be done all over again.'

20 The night wore on, the sea and wind ever rising, and the ship ever plunging more
distractedly; we shortened sail to main topsail and staysail, stopped engines and hove
to, but to little purpose. Tales of ponies down came frequently from forward, where
Oates and Atkinson laboured through the entire night. Worse was to follow, much
worse—a report from the engine-room that the pumps had choked and the water
25 risen over the gratings.

From this moment, about 4 A.M., the engine-room became the centre of interest.
The water gained in spite of every effort. Lashley, to his neck in rushing water, stuck
gamely to the work of clearing suctions. For a time, with donkey engine and bilge
pump sucking, it looked as though the water would be got under; but the hope was
30 short-lived: five minutes of pumping invariably led to the same result—a general
choking of the pumps.

The outlook appeared grim. The amount of water which was being made, with the
ship so roughly handled, was most uncertain. 'We knew that normally the ship was
not making much water, but we also knew that a considerable part of the water
35 washing over the upper deck must be finding its way below; the decks were leaking in
streams. The ship was very deeply laden; it did not need the addition of much water
to get her water-logged, in which condition anything might have happened.' The
hand pump produced only a dribble, and its suction could not be got at; as the water

40

crept higher it got in contact with the boiler and grew warmer—so hot at last that no one could work at the suctions. Williams had to confess he was beaten and must draw fires. What was to be done? Things for the moment appeared very black. The sea seemed higher than ever; it came over lee rail and poop, a rush of green water; the ship wallowed in it; a great piece of the bulwark carried clean away.

Question One: Guidance

One point to note is that the statements will come in the same order as they might appear in the text. Go slowly and work methodically through the text.

Question One: Exemplar

Read again the first part of **Source A** from **lines 1 to 14.**

Choose four statements below which are **true.**

[4 marks]

1. Kingsley returns to camp just after two o'clock.
2. The holes seem bottomless to Kingsley.
3. Kingsley knows someone who died from falling into one of the holes.
4. Kingsley and her colleagues are almost out of water.
5. They've been drinking rainwater.
6. The water supply is being stopped by the thick forest.
7. By 4.10, the camp has received water.
8. The water is delivered by men on horses.

Question Two: Guidance

In terms of structuring your response, you want to identify a difference/similarity/point (whichever the question asks for), support it with an appropriate quotation from one text, and then infer a meaning. Then move onto the other text, select a textual detail, and infer something else. If you can do this whole process a second time, you will do well – though how well you do will depend on how much detail you put into the second paragraph: to get into the Level 4 band (7-8 marks) you need to offer 'perceptive' points with detail (as opposed to 'clear', which is the marker of Level 3 (5-6 marks)).

A point on timing: this is the first long-form answer, but it is not the longest. Questions 3 and 4 are both worth more than the 8 marks up for grabs in Question 2. So remember to time yourself – roughly spend 10 minutes on this question – to ensure you have enough time to answer the other questions. Students can spend too long on Question 2, severely hampering their responses in the rest of the exam questions.

Question Two: Exemplar

You need to refer to **Source A** and **Source B** for this question.

Both of these sources describe expeditions abroad.

Write a summary of the similarities between the experiences of the explorers.

[8 marks]

*Although Source A describes an expedition to a warm forest and Source B is about an arctic trip, both show the difficulties of such exploratory trips and the dangers they pose to the explorers.[1] In Source A, the writer explains how they are nervous about 'deep holes' that have no apparent end. She is convinced 'they will be my end'. **It might be suggested that in the forest danger can be found everywhere.[2] Likewise[3]** as day turns into night in Source B the storm continues; there is no respite for these workers, especially Lashley who is up 'to his neck in rushing water' lower down in the engine room. Understandably both sets of explorers must be incredibly careful or they risk death, **whether it be in an African forest or at sea.[4]***

*In both sources, **the weather is a powerful and dangerous entity.[5]** In Source A the storm is 'hurling down lightnings and rivers of water' without consideration of those in the forest. Nature does not discriminate and threatens everyone. **Similarly[6]** in Source B a storm at sea puts everyone at risk:[7] the waves 'completely submerged' some of the workers on the ship deck. The force of the water means they have to 'cling for dear life' onto the ship's railings, implying how precarious their situation is. **In both sources, then,[8]** the explorers must be careful or they risk facing nature's wrath.*

1) From the beginning of my answer I'm comparing the extracts and suggesting a similarity. 2) I'm signalling that I'm making an inference. 3) Keywords such as 'Likewise' show that I'm identifying similarities between the sources. 4) A summative final comment that draws together both sources. 5) In this paragraph I'm discussing a theme (or 'big idea') in both sources. 6) Again, 'similarly' suggests the links between the sources. 7) I'm using the colon to provide evidence to support my point. 8) My concluding remark again emphasises the similarities between the sources.

Question Three: Guidance

Never name a technique without pausing over it in some form. Device spotting ('xx is an adverb' or 'this is a simile') will not get you marks: the exam board have repeatedly stated in their comments for both Paper One and Paper Two that terminology should only ever be used to enhance a response.

Also, it can be best to keep it simple. Focusing on an individual word and its connotations will probably prove more useful than showing an awareness of Russian formalism or narrative theory. Exploring how an individual word effects the passage is often well rewarded in the exam (although make sure you do so within the context of the passage – ensure there are textual details that support your point).

As in Question Two, use short, integrated quotations in your response. If you just quote from the text at length, your answer becomes more of a paraphrase.

Question Three: Exemplar

You now need to refer only to **Source A** from **lines 15 to 27**.

How does the writer use language to describe the weather?

[12 marks]

*1) **My introductory remark provides an overall argument for the answer.** **Also 'awesome' here means to inspire awe, not necessarily how great it is.** 2) **Again the colon precedes my quotation to support the point being made.** 3) **Providing two effects suggests how I am alert to how the writer uses language.***

***Throughout the extract the writer uses language to describe the awesome power of the storm.**[1] Kingsley uses alliteration at the paragraph's opening to introduce the 'terrific tornado', giving it a biting power. Once the storm hits, the writer uses sibilance and onomatopoeia to emphasise its power:[2] the wind has a 'shrill squeal', which suggests how unpleasant it is for those to be near the storm and hear it. The word 'squeal' also has a primal power: Kingsley thus presents nature at its most original and dangerous.*

*That the writer says the tornado is 'growling' suggests its animal-istic, primal power. This continues in the description once the storm has begun: the thunder 'roar[s]', **giving a sense of both how vicious the storm is and how loud it is**.[3] The writer also describes how the storm is 'wrapping us up', casting the storm as a snake that has caught its prey. This lexicon of animals **overall then suggests how aggressive the*** *storm is,[4] and those caught in it should seriously fear for their lives.*

*However **Kingsley**[5] also uses other schemes of reference in the extract. To suggest how loud the storm is, she likens her situation to being 'in the middle of its engine room', with the contrast of being in nature with the scene of industry suggesting the almost-unnatural or artificial power of the storm. Added to this, the writer uses a simile, 'like flights of spears among the forest trees', to describe the forks of lightening flying through the air. In this situation, it is as if humans are fighting against nature. **Finally**[6] Kingsley personifies the mountain and the storm to suggest the two are fighting: these titans of nature are at war. Kingsley thus elevates the situation throughout the extract to suggest the power of the storm.*

4) I'm tying my analysis of language together at the end of the paragraph. 5) Throughout this answer I refer to 'the writer' and 'Kingsley' – both are fine. 6) 'Finally' suggests how my answer has presented various uses of language throughout the answer.

Question Four: Guidance

There are 16 marks for the taking in Question Four, so you'll want to spend around 20 minutes on your answer. It is supposed to be demanding. Throughout your answer you will want to use comparative language (see my annotations throughout the example answers).

A Level 1 (1-4 marks) response to this question will make simple references with a few brief quotations. To not engage with the 'methods' used means to offer only a two-dimensional response. At higher levels you will have a conceptualised response to the task, meaning you explore certain ideas or perspectives (or what we might call 'themes') in relation to both writers (comparing and contrasting them, of course).

Question Four: Exemplar

For this question, you need to refer to the **whole of Source A**, together with the **whole of Source B**.

Compare how the writers convey their feelings about the challenges they face on their journeys.

In your answer, you could:

- compare their different attitudes

- compare the methods the writers use to convey their different attitudes
- support your response with references to both texts.

[16 marks]

1) From the beginning of my answer I'm comparing the sources and summarising them both in relation to the question's topic. 2) I'm using brackets in my answer to quote from the text in a way that is unobtrusive to my own point. 3) Throughout my analysis of Source B I've discussed several points, and now I'm comparing the methods in Source A. 4) My language shows how I'm ranging throughout the source. 5) Here I'm directly comparing structural points. 6) Throughout the answer I adopt a comparative approach. 7) I'm using brackets here to add an extra point of comparison that is focused on methods. 8) My use of references are specific without needlessly quoting from the text.

Whilst Kingsley suggests an excitement to the challenges she faced during her journey, Scott's diary bristles with a fear of the situation that he's in.[1] *From the beginning of Source B, Scott uses* **the short sentence** *'A day of great disaster' to set the concerned tone and establish a foreboding atmosphere. From there, Scott's use of technical language* **('topsails, jib, and staysails')**[2] *implies the skill of the men, but they cannot do enough to fully fight the 'onslaught' caused by the storm. Scott's word choice suggests the grand severity of the situation. Other words, such as the 'plunging' ship, and phrases, such as how the men had to 'cling for dear life', suggests how the men can barely survive.* **Source A also uses specific words**[3] *for effect to emphasise Kingsley's difficulties in the forest: she has to 'heave' rocks into the bottomless holes, but does not hear the onomatopoeic 'splash'. But the humorous hyperbole that these holes 'will by my end' does add a slightly joking tone to the source* **before Kingsley goes on, later,**[4] *to describe the dangerous storm.*

Once the storm begins in Source A, 'cascades' of rushing water pass down the mountain, with Kingsley using a long sentence to capture its rushing power. **Equally, the dramatic short sentence**[5] *'The outlook appeared grim' in Source B shows Scott's fear and concern.* **But where Kingsley's tone is one of awe at nature's power, Scott often suggests not only his fear but also that of his colleagues.**[6] *Scott's reference to his fellow shipmen (such as Williams, Oates and Atkinson) humanises the writing, reminding readers of the lives that might easily be lost. On Scott's ship, everything threatens the sailors: items 'began to break loose', which requires the men to fight against their cargo. They are 'heaving coal sacks overboard'* **(like Kingsley, 'heaving' suggests their exertion)**[7] *and 're-lashing the petrol cases'. Against this exciting description, Kingsley's documenting of the times in* **the second paragraph of Source A**[8] *seems rather tame. Nonetheless, Kingsley's text does record her group's desire for water (somewhat ironically, the later storm provides plenty). Tracing every thirty minutes (and sometimes even shorter intervals), Kingsley reminds readers that even the most basic of supplies can be difficult to source when in an African forest.*

Both writers use a language of battle to suggest the challenges of their expeditions.[9] *For example, in Source A Kingsley personifies the storm and the mountain to set the two in opposition. 'Mungo' the mountain 'growls and swears' at the storm, which is met by an aggressive 'hurling down' of lightning and rain. Kingsley thus casts both the mountain and the storm as primordial beings ready to fight, and she is trapped in between such forces of power. This is symbolically represented when the fire, a man-made thing, is extinguished although it 'fought a good fight'. Likewise Scott's diary suggests a battle between man and nature, with the latter decisively winning. The crashing waves means the coal-bags are 'like battering rams', with* **Scott's simile implying the weighty power**[10] *they've accrued at sea. Meanwhile in the engine room the pump produces 'only a dribble', with Scott's word choice implying the pathetic failure of the machinery to fight against the storm. In spite of the efforts of the seamen, they are eventually 'beaten'.* **As suggested in both sources, some challenges evidently prove too great for man.**[11]

*9) **A comparative point directly related to the question that introduces the theme of the paragraph. 10) Each technique is matched with an observation. 11) My final line just secures me some final AO3 marks by summatively concluding how both sources can be linked to the question.***

A photo from Sierra Leone taken in 1891 — two years prior to Kingsley's account!

A difficult situation...

SECTION B: WRITING

Question Five: Guidance

If you've read Accolade's book on Paper One, you'll know that I try to make Question Five a do-able challenge. Again I want to encourage you to think of this task as something that you can prepare for during your studies and revision. To begin with, you will need to consider the purpose, audience and form of your work. The forms you might be expected to write in can include: letters, autobiography, articles, speeches, diary entries, sketches, magazine articles. The list goes on and can include any non-fiction or literary non-fiction genre. You will be told which form your answer must take, and you will be given the purpose of the work (you might have to explain, argue, advise, persuade or educate).

As for the audience, that's where you've got to pause and think. Who will be receiving this work? How would you address your headmaster (say, in a letter) and how does this compare to the ways you would speak with your friends or school peers (for example, during a speech)? More broadly, how would you grab the attention of someone in, maybe, a newspaper article? Being aware of your audience and tailoring your response accordingly is what's referred to in the AO5 mark scheme as being 'convincing'.

Producing a clear argument will get you into Level 3. Use signposting to help the examiner gauge which direction your work is heading in. Think of your argument as a journey and just like any trip we need signs to guide us to our destination. Certain phrases or words (such as 'Consequently', 'As a result',

'Alternatively', 'Furthermore', 'Additionally') can make it clear to the reader how each paragraph is going to contribute to your argument, but they must be used in the right context: for example, 'However' signals a counter-argument is about to be made. On this topic, be very cautious about introducing a counter-argument to your work – it may well de-rail your own argument and leave your response not consistent with your ideas. To deal with this, have a counter to your counter-argument that overall strengthens your argument – this will be tricky, but it will really show a maturity of thought, expression and argument.

Think also about the structure of your work. Remember in Paper One how that pesky Question Three is all about how structure is used to **interest** you as a reader? Well, now it's time for you to use that knowledge in your answer: you need to be using structure to interest your audience!

Other features you might want to make use of, where applicable, can include: puns, rhetorical features, extended metaphors, hyperbole, imagery, analogy, and symbolism. To ensure your work is well-suited to your audience, you can spend some time before the exam considering which features are best suited to each form. Using features not well suited to the task – for example, you wouldn't use sub-headings in a diary entry or imagery in a factual newspaper article – can risk your answer being classed as not strictly understanding the form or audience required.

If at this point the thought of writing your Question 5 responses in a way that uses structure and literary features for effect with a strong argument (and, maybe, a counter-argument) is a bit much, then **planning** your answers will be the way forward. Planning will help marshal your thoughts and it will perhaps help you identify which techniques to put where. Planning also stops you from writing too much (quality is preferred over quantity) and it gives your hand a little break from all that writing. It will let you think through the structure of your work and will hopefully give you an overview of your argument. You only want to spend five minutes planning (you need to have enough time to actually write your response!). If possible, factor in some editing time at the end to check over your spelling, punctuation and grammar to secure those top AO6 marks. Planning can also be a great way of revising for this exam: find an example of a Question 5 topic and plan your response: you'll be engaging all the right mental muscles!

Finally, and this can be easily forgotten, try to respond to the task with enthusiasm and confidence. These questions are meant to prompt a strong opinion, and you're expected to back this up. So long as it's focused, there is no wrong answer for this question, so really go for it!

Now you're not expected to be able to call to mind statistics on internet safety, the history of your school or any other scenario you might be asked to write about.

You can, however make up statistics or expert opinions. But, a word of caution about this: the exam board have suggested it's best to use a well-placed literary technique or structural choice for effect, as these features are more likely to effectively support your argument. Also ensure your ideas are detailed.

Question Five: Exemplar

'It's only when people are pushed to their limits that they do their best work.'

Write a diary entry that explores a time when you faced a difficult situation.

**(24 marks for content and organisation
16 marks for technical accuracy)
[40 marks]**

Dear Diary,

I cannot believe what happened today. [1]

I've been helping out at church now for the past three months. Every week I help collect the money, hand out newsletters and act as an usher. I'm not saying I'm indispensable but I like trying to support my local community: sometimes you might be the only person that an older member of the congregation speaks to that week. I also think it's vital that young people are involved in their communities: **too often are we evoked as being irresponsible, uncaring and selfish.** [2]

But for some people, the idea of young people being involved **is like some kind of crime.** [3] *I was told today that one* **'church goer'** *has, in fact, complained about my helping out; apparently I'm* **'too young'.** [4]

Frankly, it's ridiculous. [5] *I know I'm only sixteen, but who is he to say who should and should not help out in church? For a start, isn't the whole point of going to church that you're meant to not judge others?* [6] *That certainly was one of the commandments...*

It's people like this man that **perpetuate** *the myth that young people are awful without providing them any opportunity to defend themselves. Being a teenager is* **a constant battle:** [7] *if you're not critiquing yourself, you're being critiqued by your peers. If not*

1) **A short, dramatic sentence to grab my reader's attention. Note how my sentences are short and clear. While the occasional (well executed!) complicated sentence can impress, generally you are best off keeping it simple: it's difficult to maintain accurate punctuation and grammar across longer sentences. 2)** *I'm also invoking wider social observations, to add a sense of power to my work.* *3)* **A simple, effective simile. 4)** *I'm using apostrophes here in two ways: the first to highlight the hypocrisy of the 'church goer' complaining about someone being helpful; the second is a quotation of what the man said. 5)* **Short sentence to start the next paragraph with a bit of anger.**

*6) **Rhetorical questions and ellipses add a contemplative mood to this paragraph.** 7) **A metaphorical battle, of course.** 8) **Throughout this paragraph I'm using higher-level vocabulary.** 9) **Note my use of the semicolon, a high-level piece of vocabulary.** 10) **Brackets here add extra detail to my paragraph. They can also be used to show character and overall they contribute to the tone of your work.** 11) **Notice how throughout my answer I've used paragraphs for effect – it's a tightly organised response. You can only really achieve this through planning and thinking exactly about what you want to say.** 12) **A short, declarative sentence that brims with passion – a good way to get your examiner on side!***

*them, then there is always someone else willing to jump in and remind us how awful we are. Worse still, the media has a **vendetta** against us: we're lazy, entitled, fussy, and overly concerned with things that don't matter. 'Young adult' is a term of **condescension**,[8] not maturity. To be 'woke' is now to be misguided, not accepting or appreciative of other people's perspectives and ideas. It's exhausting to have my daily existence questioned by older people who think they have a right to judge us all the time.*

However, I shouldn't let one man taint my experiences. The weekly conversations, the 'Hiya love', and the warm smiles on a cold evening all make it worth while. I believe in taking every opportunity and not being deterred by anyone;[9] only when pushing oneself in the face of adversity both big and small can we improve and do good.

*I don't think I'll ever change his mind, but I can outwardly prove him wrong. Aside from saying the mass itself, I can become a reader **(suggesting not all young people use 'like' in every other sentence)**,[10] I can help teach the younger members of the community, and I can start taking part in the weekly soup kitchen.*

Some good can come in the face of adversity and if others benefit from my proving this guy wrong, then even better.[11]

All things considered, I've rarely been placed in a difficult situation in my life. But in the face of unfounded discrimination, I know it's time to stand up and do something.

***Until then, I must not let him get me down.**[12]*

Sample Paper Three

Samuel Morse, 1840.

Cutting-Edge Technologies: The Daguerreotype & Virtual Reality

Source A: *A daguerreotype was one of the first photographic processes that saw high-quality images printed onto copper plates. In Source A, a letter printed in the New-York Observer in April 1839, Professor Samuel F. B. Morse records a visit to Louis J. M. Daguerre, the inventor of the process that created these new prints.*

1 "They are produced on a metallic surface, the principal pieces about 7 inches by 5, and they resemble aquatint engravings, for they are in simple chiaro oscuro, and not in colors. But the exquisite minuteness of the delineation cannot be conceived. No painting or engraving ever approached it. For example: In a view up the street, a
5 distant sign would be perceived, and the eye could just discern that there were lines of letters upon it, but so minute as not to be read with the naked eye. By the assistance of a powerful lens, which magnified 50 times, applied to the delineation, every letter was clearly and distinctly legible, and also were the minutest breaks and lines in the walls of the buildings, and the pavements of the street. The effect of the
10 lens upon the picture was in a great degree like that of the telescope in nature.

"Objects moving are not impressed. The Boulevard, so constantly filled with a moving throng of pedestrians and carriages, was perfectly solitary, except an individual who was having his boots brushed. His feet were compelled, of course, to be stationary for some time, one being on the box of the boot-black, and the other on
15 the ground. Consequently, his boots and legs are well defined, but he is without body or head because these were in motion.

The impressions of interior views are Rembrandt perfected. One of Mr. D.'s plates is an impression of a spider. The spider was not bigger than the head of a large pin, but the image, magnified by the solar microscope to the size of the palm of the hand, having been impressed on the plate, and examined through a lens, was further magnified, and showed a minuteness of organization hitherto not seen to exist. You perceive how this discovery is, therefore, about to open a new field of research in the depths of microscopic nature. We are soon to see if the minute has discoverable limits. The naturalist is to have a new kingdom to explore, as much beyond the microscope as the microscope is beyond the naked eye.

But I am near the end of my paper, and I have unhappily to give a melancholy close to my account of this ingenious discovery. M. Daguerre appointed yesterday at noon to see my telegraph. He came, and passed more than an hour with me, expressing himself highly gratified at its operation. But while he was thus employed the great building of the Diorama, with his own house, all his beautiful works, his valuable notes and papers, the labor of years of experiment, were, unknown to him, at that moment becoming the prey of the flames. His secret indeed is still safe with him, but the steps of his progress in the discovery, and his valuable researches in science, are lost to the scientific world. I learn that his Diorama was insured, but to what extent I know not. I am sure all friends of science and improvement will unite in expressing the deepest sympathy in M. Daguerre's loss, and the sincere hope that such a liberal sum will be awarded him by his Government, as shall enable him in some degree at least, to recover from his loss.

───────────────

Source B: Although virtual reality (VR) has been in development since the twentieth century, it is only recently that it has been made more readily available to the general public. In the article below, Ka Bradley explores how, during the COVID-19 pandemic, VR technology has become a vital part of the arts industry.

───────────────

1   It's fortunately possible to think of the BFI London Film Festival's new virtual and augmented reality strand, LFF Expanded, as innovative engagement with the medium of film in and of its own right, rather than *only* a way of adjusting to this terrible new reality where theatres close and audiences shrink and jobs are cut.
5   Though it might be difficult to look at film and performance with optimism right now, LFF Expanded's programme assures us that boundaries are still being tested, play and curiosity and experimentation are still supported in a time of uncertainty. That virtual reality and film can also be beamed directly into the living rooms, bedrooms and home offices of audiences is relevant and cheering: we continue to be
10   an audience, together apart.

We are at the very start of the age of virtual and augmented reality: the technology exists, but sometimes at glitching, counterintuitive or superfluous levels. (In ten years, we might look at the helmet-like headsets the way we now look at 1980s brick-thick carphones.) When VR works, viewers come away with a real sense of having witnessed the crystallisation of a new art form. When it doesn't, it can feel baffling or frustrating, making grouchy Luddites* out of the most tech-savvy.

Fortunately, the Expanded strand has some inspiring examples of how new technology might work in service of dance and performance. This was striking in the 360° film *Gimme One*. A 360° film differs from VR and AR in that it does not promise an augmented layer on top of our reality, nor does it plunge us into a box-fresh coded reality outside of our own. It is, simply, a film that you sit within, rather than one which you face on a screen – a basic benchmark for 'immersive' theatre.

Gimme One is a documentary film about British ballroom culture – focusing on London and Bristol – and in some respects has some conventional documentary frameworks. Talking heads (members of the ballroom community) describe their personal experience of vogueing, of the 'houses' they belong to, of the ways the ballroom community has encouraged them to explore and accept their gender identities and sexualities. Their first-person descriptions are interspersed with filmed fragments from vogue balls, and with stylised, computer-rendered neon silhouettes of vogueing dancers against depthless VR black. As with the Expanded thread's other 360° films, at-home audiences can experience *Gimme One* at home on YouTube.

The VR format, however, does something that feels special. Those talking heads appear as real people sitting in front of us, making eye contact, laughing in conversation and – though our part of the script is silent – this makes their private revelations feel much more intimate. This film was put together with the engaged collaboration of its performers; our ability to face and greet these performers emphasises this personal connection. Teleported into a nightclub, we sit in the midst of the audience to watch the dancers walk (as vogueing across a strip of dance floor is known); it's impossible to contain a surge of tenderness and nostalgia for crowds we've sat in, nightclubs we've drunk at, people we're been crammed with, shoulder to shoulder. Hip-deep in revellers – the floor levels can take a bit of adjustment – I thought about my friends who have been felled by post-viral chronic exhaustion, who suffer from anxiety in crowded spaces, who live far away from centres of queer culture but long to be immersed in it. This technology is in its infancy, and cannot replicate interaction, but its initial forays into recording the buzz of the world feel optimistic.

*A Luddite is a person opposed to new technology or new ways of thinking.

Ka Bradley's 'Dancing virtually into the London Film Festival' (27/10/2020) was reproduced courtesy of Springback Magazine.

Question One: Guidance

Whilst many students tend to do well with this question, there is a significant number of students that do not follow the instructions, meaning they then lose marks. Shade the circles, do *not* write 'T' or 'F' next to the statement for 'True' or 'False' respectively, and if you make an error ensure you clearly cross out the whole box. Some students circle more than four answers; examiners, however, will take away one mark for every extra statement identified.

Notice below how the wrong answers deliberately use information from the source – you'll have to read it carefully in the exam to not make any silly errors!

Question One: Exemplar

Read again the first part of **Source B** from **lines 1 to 16.**

Choose four statements below which are **true.**

[4 marks]

1. LFF is part of a new virtual reality strand.
2. It is only on for two weeks.
3. Restrictions mean it's difficult to think positively about performances.
4. The LFF strand is not only restricted to theatres.
5. The predecessor to the headsets was the 1980s carphones.
6. The technology is flawless.
7. Virtual reality technology still has mixed results.
8. Some people, called Luddites, worship this new technology.

Question Two: Guidance

Remember to make sure you understand the specific topic or focus of the question set: a number of Examiner's Reports for this question have noted that students often write about the wrong topic or theme in the extracts. Also, simply noting the two texts are from different time periods is not enough; you might want to use this as a point of comparison about the ideas presented in the text, however to discuss the context behind these works is not necessary at all.

You need to refer to **Source A** and **Source B** for this question.

Both of these sources describe new technology.

Write a summary of the differences between the Daguerreotype and VR technology.

[8 marks]

Both sources were written in very different times, and as such the differences between the Daguerreotype and VR technology are pronounced.[1] *Although the writer in Source A is optimistic about the future the daguerreotype will have on scientific observation, it is still a developing technology. For example, that the picture of the man is 'without body or head because these were in motion'* **indicates how the object is yet to be able to fully process movement.**[2] *At present, this technology is not quite fully fit for human use, for it would require everyone to stay still whilst having their photograph taken. Source B, however, is explicitly about how VR Technology can capture dance performance. Because of this technology, we can 'face and greet' the performers and visualise them properly.* **It's a far cry from the headless bodies created by the daguerreotype.**[3]

VR also has a much wider potential to be viewed: it can be seen in 'living rooms, bedrooms and home officers',overall creating an audience that is, as the writer suggests, 'together apart'.[4] *Moreover VR Technology can be watched on YouTube, meaning it can be experienced anywhere and on the move, whereas the daguerreotype is produced on small 'principal pieces'.* **At the end of Source A**[5] *the writer explains how the fire in Mr Daguerre's home destroys the research. Years of work at that moment are lost, as was its potential at that moment to revolutionise scientific enquiry.* **Thus where Source B suggests how VR Technology, once online, is theoretically safe and secure, Source A reminds us**[6] *of how precious and fragile earlier scientific work was, with years of research potentially gone with the lighting of a flame.*

1) My opening sentence always sets out my argument for the answer. 2) Here's an example of me making an inference based on the text. 3) Here I am implicitly contrasting both technologies. 4) Note how my quotations are short and integrated; I am also combining inference with detail. 5) Again my language here suggests how I am ranging throughout the source. 6) Note again my use of comparison throughout the source – every point on one source is matched with one from the other.

Question Three: Guidance

You will be given a specific part of one of the sources to analyse, so stay within those boundaries. Students also struggle because they outline instead of analyse (remember this question is about suggesting the effect of language) and they over-analyse the use of colour (sometimes the curtains are just blue!). The main issue for students with this sort of question, however, is device spotting: I cannot emphasise enough that you must go beyond simply listing techniques. You must always also comment on effect.

Question Three: Exemplar

You now need to refer only to **Source A** from **lines 11 to 25**.

How does the writer use language to describe the pictures?

[12 marks]

1) My writing is always focused on 'the writer' – referring to the text in this way shows you're aware of AO2 automatically... 2) ... and again... 3) ...and again – my use of 'moreover' here adds the suggestion that I am comprehensively analysing the text. 4) A short, simple sentence to show my comprehension. 5) Recognising and writing about tone is difficult; but, if you can, it shows how engaged you are with the text. 6) Note how throughout my answer to this question I detailed both pictures and then drew everything together. This way I'm engaging with the extract in its entirety: having a structure where you work through the extract can often be the best way to approach these sorts of questions.

Throughout the extract the writer suggests how the pictures are impressive yet there are still faults to be found. Describing the first picture, the writer describes the 'throng of pedestrians and carriages', with the word 'throng' indicating the mass of people present in the Boulevard. **From there the writer focuses**[1] *on a single man who is having his 'boots brushed', with the alliteration adding a determined feeling to these boots. This use of alliteration continues when* **the writer**[2] *describes how one foot was on the 'box of boot-black' for the shoe polishing.* **Moreover the writer**[3] *personifies the feet by suggesting they were 'compelled' to be stationary, suggesting how the picture captures the inactivity of the foot.*

In the second picture the writer describes a spider.[4] *In spite of noting how the spider 'was not bigger than the head of a large pin', through the magnification the writer now appears to be the 'size of the palm of the hand'.* **The awed tone**[5] *throughout the paragraph adds to how revolutionary the pictures are (they show 'a minuteness of organisation hitherto not seen to exist'), which is emphasised by the repetition of 'magnified'.*

There is a hyperbolic celebration throughout the extract prompted by the daguerreotype. This is fully captured in the metaphorical idea that, because of this technology, the naturalist will have 'a new kingdom to explore'. The writer's metaphor suggests how, because of these pictures that show the potential of this new technology, naturalists can now go on almost heroic quests to discover what else has been so-far hidden from the 'naked eye'. **Thus the writer uses language to celebrate the quality of** *the pictures and the potential they have for scientific research in the future.*[6]

Question Four: Guidance

One thing to remember for this question is that you need to write about the writer's ideas. Keep your answers focused on the writer, otherwise you risk your mark being capped in Level 2 (5-8 marks). Students have also struggled because they forget to write about methods: hopefully it's clear by now why this is such a bad idea. The how (the methods) are as important as the what (the ideas).

Question Four: Exemplar

For this question, you need to refer to the **whole of Source A**, together with the **whole of Source B**.

Compare how the writers convey their attitudes about the potential that new technology will have in their fields of work.

In your answer, you could:

- compare their different attitudes
- compare the methods the writers use to convey their different attitudes
- support your response with references to both texts.

[16 marks]

1) My opening sentence summarises the argument I'm going to use throughout my answer. 2) Well-chosen verbs can show your comprehension of the work.

In spite of any limitations, both writers are understandably excited about the potential the new technology they discuss will have in their fields.[1]

*Throughout Source A the writer stresses how revolutionary this new technology is. This extends to the praise he **lavishes**[2] on the 'exquisite minuteness' of the work, indicating the quality of the picture; this is confirmed in the short sentence 'No painting or engraving ever approached it.' The writer here uses a short sentence to portray the significance of this new work. Likewise Source B captures the writer's excitement at what the new technology means for dance and performance. This is captured in the **oxymoron** 'together apart' to describe how VR technology can support the LFF Expanded research strand. **In placing this observation at the end of the paragraph,**[3] Bradley adds*

emphasis to this observation, posing it as the technology's greatest success. The grandeur of observing 'We are at the very start of the age of virtual and augmented reality' implies this new technology is as important as the Stone or Iron ages, which saw developments in civilisation across the world.

Both sources[4] *convey an excitement for what this research will mean for the future. Throughout Source B the writer uses lists to demonstrate how much the VR technology can display and the ways in which it can be accessed. The talking heads, for example, make eye contact, laugh and 'converse' with the viewer, creating a life-like experience.* **The suggestion that VR technology represents a 'crystallisation of a new art form' adds both a beauty and a hardness to this work.**[5] *The potential of VR technology means that when used one might find oneself 'Teleported into a nightclub', with the writer's use of 'teleported' implying not only the ease and lack of boundaries but also the futuristic power it will have in the future. Again there is an optimism throughout Source A that this 'discovery', which itself imbues the pictures with a mythical dimension, will 'open a new field of research'. This idea of 'opening' out suggests the ways in which research leads to more research; presumably, at the end of this process, we will reach a better world.* **This optimism is expressed in both texts.**[6]

Yet both sources conclude with a different focus.[7] *The writer in Source B does note how this technology still has some ways to go. She personifies the technology when writing how it is still 'in its infancy', yet there is still much room to grow. Regardless, VR technology has created a 'buzz', a word brimming with onomatopoeic excitement. The conclusion of Source B is a stark contrast to that of Source A, which reveals how the new technology has been destroyed by the fire.* **That the work is 'prey of the flames' metaphorically emphasises how susceptible it was to being damaged, a stark reminder today of how vulnerable research physically was before the digital age; the word 'prey' casts the research as something vulnerable.**[8] *At the end of the article, the writer hopes Mr Daguerre will receive some financial recompense to help him 'recover from his loss.' In personifying the research as a loved one, the writer emphasises the emotional significance of the work to the researcher. Like any family member, its loss is something to be mourned. Both sources overall show how scientific developments can alter our everyday life – it is unsurprising, then, that the writer of Source A should frame the destruction of research as a tragic event.*

*3) **Analysis of both language and structure is encouraged throughout your answer to Question 4.** 4) **My answers throughout this guide might seem repetitive, but why complicate it? You want your language to show the ways in which you're answering the question.** 5) **Exploring two meanings suggests how I'm alert to the use of language.** 6) **My concluding line just ties all of my analysis back to the main point of the paragraph. Using themes in this way can ensure you're comparing the texts.** 7) **Focusing on the end of a text is always a nice way of bringing your analysis together.** 8) **Here I'm both analysing the text and drawing out wider meanings.***

A woman wearing a virtual reality headset. Copyright © University of Texas at Austin

Should we be thankful for technology?

SECTION B: WRITING

Question Five: Guidance

Contrary to what you might expect, it is often the students that write pages and pages of material that can suffer. This is because over that sustained period the accuracy of their writing (in terms of spelling, punctuation and grammar) dips, meaning they lose marks for AO6 (being able to maintain the accuracy of your work is what distinguished Level 3 responses (which are 'mostly' accurate) from Level 2 ones (which are 'sometimes' accurate)). Also note how you must employ a 'sophisticated' vocabulary to get into Level 3 in AO6: even if accurate, if your spelling is basic it is not significantly fulfilling the mark scheme.

Students can also struggle with the accuracy of their punctuation. Colons and semi-colons especially can prove troublesome; so, to combat this, I'd suggest you spend some time revisiting the rules behind using these pieces of punctuation and then write some practice sentences that use them accurately. Practice makes perfect!

Question Five: Exemplar

'We should be thankful for how quickly technology is developing today – without it, we wouldn't be able to live our lives so efficiently.'

Write a letter to the editor of a newspaper in which you argue your point of view in response to this statement.

**(24 marks for content and organisation
16 marks for technical accuracy)
[40 marks]**

Dear Editor,[1]

Last week I read of how one individual was extolling the virtues of new technology owing to its efficiency. Yet where they celebrated these developments, **I found myself thinking more about the downfalls of a world that is reliant on technology***.*

I'm increasingly saddened by the ways in which our society wants to make things more 'efficient' **because it is apparent that all we are becoming is lazy***.*[2]

Why are people so busy that they need to use contactless instead of press five buttons on a pin machine? Why walk to a takeaway when it can be delivered? Why learn to spell when autocorrect can correct every **foible** *and suggest unlimited synonyms?*[3]

I shudder to think where we will be in twenty years' time. For a start, we'll probably all be obese:[4] *instead of going for a walk, we can wear a headset for a virtual jaunt around a nature reserve before ordering a takeaway to be delivered as a reward for 'getting out'.* **Efficient? Yes. Good for us? Absolutely not.**[5]

Aside from the **numbing** *effects of technology, it has also been* **hampering**[6] *our society. Because of social media, generations of young people must now* **combat**[7] *impossible standards of beauty, wealth and fitness. The world is supposed to be more connected with technology, but you cannot engage in a proper conversation with your face squashed up against a* **luminescent**[8] *screen.*

Look also at the demise of the high street. Yes, your pair of jeans or your LEGO set can be with you tomorrow, but spare a thought for the independent businesses who are closing down daily. Imagine a world without shops or restaurants;[9] *high-streets will become* **hives that expel**[10] *couriers into the night to deal with our various wishes within ten minutes if we continue to put our own needs before those of others.*

1) **This is a letter to a newspaper editor, so the full address (etc) is not needed, but nonetheless a formal introduction is used.** *2)* **I'm using these opening paragraphs to make my view clear.** *3)* **A paragraph of questions to get my reader thinking the same way as me. A 'foible' is a minor error, but it also applies to eccentricity.** *4)* **I'm using a colon to add detail to my point.** *5)* **I've here used hypophora (where you pose a question and then answer it immediately) for effect, which is emphasised further by my use of short sentences.** *6)* **A vocabulary that implies the negative impact of technology. Notice also how I'm tying the topic into 'big ideas'.** *7)* **'combat' implies it's a war.** *8)* **A well-placed adjective can really add character to your work.** *9)* **The semi-colon connects two sentences that are linked by topic.** *10)* **Where 'hives' suggests insects, 'expel' adds an unnatural feeling to this vision of the future.**

Instead, might I suggest that we all take a step back and slow down?[11]

Let's just learn to enjoy things more and be happier with simpler things: for generations we made do without computers and gadgets. Children today would be horrified to learn that, before PlayStations and IPhones, a stick and a hoola hoop were responsible for hours of fun. **A terrifying thought, I know.**[12]

Let's[13] *teach our children that they do not need this or that thing straight away.* **Let's** *teach them the importance of patience and of value.* **Let's**[14] *teach them that the world is there solely to satisfy them.*

We have become consumed with being consumers.[15] *But the good news is that it's not too late to change: get out, walk around, read a book. You might surprise yourself with how beautiful it is out there.*

Yours sincerely,

Efficiently fed-up.[16]

11) A paragraph with a question signalling a slight change in focus. 12) Irony can really add personality to your writing. 13) Contractions, which are used throughout this response, add a slightly informal tone. 14) Notice how I'm using the same sentence opening to add increasing emphasis to the points I'm making — this technique is called anaphora and it's a great little tactic to get someone to think like you do as it allows you to build up lots of rhetorical flourishes. 15) A pun on the word 'consumer'. 16) A snappy closing remark that turns the original statement on itself.

Most broadsheet newspapers contain a 'Letters to the Editor' section. These are definitely worthwhile reading while prepping for Question Five! Copyright © VV Nincic

Sample Paper Four

For the past three sample papers, I have annotated my responses so you can see how my answers correspond to the Assessment Objectives that are used to mark your answers. We've included a final sample set of answers below, and now it's time for you to annotate them yourself. Revise what each assessment objective is looking for, and then be alert to how each question is answered.

Lewisham Hospital in London — formerly, Lewisham Workhouse. Copyright © Reading Tom

Inhospitable Spaces: The Coal Mine & The Workhouse

Source A: *Following the Industrial Revolution, the demand for coal in Britain was great. However the conditions for the workers who had to work in the coal mines were often difficult and dangerous; George Orwell's essay 'Down the Mine', first published in 1937, explores this topic.*

---

1   When you go down a coal-mine it is important to try and get to the coal face when the 'fillers' are at work. This is not easy, because when the mine is working visitors are a nuisance and are not encouraged, but if you go at any other time, it is possible to come away with a totally wrong impression. On a Sunday, for instance, a mine seems
5   almost peaceful. The time to go there is when the machines are roaring and the air is black with coal dust, and when you can actually see what the miners have to do. At those times the place is like hell, or at any rate like my own mental picture of hell. Most of the things one imagines in hell are there – heat, noise, confusion, darkness, foul air, and, above all, unbearably cramped space. Everything except the fire, for
10   there is no fire down there except the feeble beams of Davy lamps and electric torches which scarcely penetrate the clouds of coal dust.

When you have finally got there – and getting there is a job in itself: I will explain that in a moment – you crawl through the last line of pit props and see opposite you a shiny black wall three or four feet high. This is the coal face. Overhead is the smooth
15   ceiling made by the rock from which the coal has been cut; underneath is the rock again, so that the gallery you are in is only as high as the ledge of coal itself, probably not much more than a yard. The first impression of all, overmastering everything else for a while, is the frightful, deafening din from the conveyor belt which carries the

coal away. You cannot see very far, because the fog of coal dust throws back the beam
20 of your lamp, but you can see on either side of you the line of half-naked kneeling
men, one to every four or five yards, driving their shovels under the fallen coal and
flinging it swiftly over their left shoulders. They are feeding it on to the conveyor belt,
a moving rubber belt a couple of feet wide which runs a yard or two behind them.
Down this belt a glittering river of coal races constantly. In a big mine it is carrying
25 away several tons of coal every minute. It bears it off to some place in the main roads
where it is shot into tubs holding half a ton, and thence dragged to the cages and
hoisted to the outer air.

It is impossible to watch the 'fillers' at work without feeling a pang of envy for their
toughness. It is a dreadful job that they do, an almost superhuman job by the stan-
30 dard of an ordinary person. For they are not only shifting monstrous quantities of
coal, they are also doing it in a position that doubles or trebles the work. They have
got to remain kneeling all the while – they could hardly rise from their knees without
hitting the ceiling – and you can easily see by trying it what a tremendous effort this
means. Shovelling is comparatively easy when you are standing up, because you can
35 use your knee and thigh to drive the shovel along; kneeling down, the whole of the
strain is thrown upon your arm and belly muscles. And the other conditions do not
exactly make things easier. There is the heat – it varies, but in some mines it is suffocating – and the coal dust that stuffs up your throat and nostrils and collects along
your eyelids, and he unending rattle of the conveyor belt, which in that confined
40 space is rather like the rattle of a machine gun. But the fillers look and work as
though they were made of iron. They really do look like iron-hammered iron statues
– under the smooth coat of coal dust which clings to them from head to foot. It is
only when you see miners down the mine and naked that you realise what splendid
men they are. Most of them are small (big men are at a disadvantage in that job) but
45 nearly all of them have the most noble bodies; wide shoulders tapering to slender
supple waits, and small pronounced buttocks and sinewy thighs, with not an ounce of
waste flesh anywhere.

Source B: *From March 1850 until May 1859 Charles Dickens published the weekly two-penny
magazine Household Words. In 'A Walk in a Workhouse' Dickens describes the conditions of a
Victorian era workhouse – workhouses were for people with no money or home, for orphaned and
abandoned children, the elderly, the disabled and the mentally and physically sick.*

---

1   When the service was over, I walked with the humane and conscientious gentleman
whose duty it was to take that walk, that Sunday morning, through the little world of
poverty enclosed within the workhouse walls. It was inhabited by a population of

some fifteen hundred or two thousand paupers, ranging from the infant newly born
or not yet come to the pauper world, to the old man dying on his bed.

In a room opening from a squalid yard, where a number of listless women were
lounging to and fro, trying to get warm in the ineffectual sunshine of the tardy May
morning – in the 'Itch Ward,' not to compromise the truth – a woman such as
HOGARTH has often drawn, was hurriedly getting on her gown before a dusty fire.
She was the nurse, or wardswoman, of that insalubrious department – herself a
pauper – flabby, raw-boned, untidy – unpromising and coarse of aspect as need be.
But, on being spoken to about the patients whom she had in charge, she turned
round, with her shabby gown half on, half off, and fell a crying with all her might.
Not for show, not querulously, not in any mawkish sentiment, but in the deep grief
and affliction of her heart; turning away her dishevelled head: sobbing most bitterly,
wringing her hands, and letting fall abundance of great tears, that choked her utter-
ance. What was the matter with the nurse of the itch-ward? O, 'the dropped child
was dead! Oh, the child that was found in the street, and she had brought up ever
since, had died an hour ago, and see where the little creature lay, beneath this cloth!
The dear, the pretty dear!

The dropped child seemed too small and poor a thing for Death to be in earnest
with, but Death had taken it; and already its diminutive form was neatly washed,
composed, and stretched as if in sleep upon a box. I thought I heard a voice from
Heaven saying, It shall be well for thee, O nurse of the itch-ward, when some less
gentle pauper does those offices to thy cold form, that such as the dropped child are
the angles who behold my Father's face!

In another room, were several ugly old women crouching, witch-like round a hearth,
and chattering and nodding, after the manner of the monkeys. 'All well here? And
enough to eat?' A general chattering and chuckling; at last an answer from a volun-
teer. 'Oh yes, gentleman! Bless you, gentleman! Lord bless the Parish of St. So-and-
So, and thankee, gentleman!' Elsewhere, a party of pauper nurses were at dinner.
'How do YOU get on?' 'Oh pretty well, sir! We works hard, and we lives hard – like
the sodgers!'

In another room, a kind of purgatory or place of transition, six or eight noisy
madwomen were gathered together, under the superintendence of one sane atten-
dant. Among them was a girl of two or three and twenty, very prettily dressed, of
most respectable appearance and good manners, who had been brought in from the
house where she had lived as a domestic servant (having, I suppose, no friends), on
account of being subject to epileptic fits, and requiring to be removed under the
influence of a very bad one. She was by no means of the same stuff, or the same
breeding, or the same experience, or in the same state of mind, as those by whom she
was surrounded; and she pathetically complained that the daily association and the
nightly noise made her worse, and was driving her mad – which was perfectly

45 evidence. The case was noted for inquiry and redress, but she said she had already been there some weeks.'

Question One: Exemplar

Read again the first part of **Source A** from **lines 1 to 11.**

Choose four statements below which are **true.**

[4 marks]

1. Visitors to the mine are always considered a nuisance. ☐
2. It is possible to visit the mine at any time. ■
3. Comparatively little work happens at a mine on Sundays. ■
4. The best day to go down a mine is on a Sunday. ☐
5. The mine makes the speaker think of hell. ■
6. There is very little space in the mine. ■
7. The mine is a well-lit environment. ☐
8. The speaker works down the mines. ☐

Question Two: Exemplar

You need to refer to **Source A** and **Source B** for this question.

Both of these sources describe difficult, unpleasant environments.

Write a summary of what you understand about these spaces.

[8 marks]

Both Dickens and Orwell emphasise how unpleasant the workhouse and coal mine are respectively. In Source A, the machines are noted as 'roaring', suggesting how loud they are. It is described how a visitor to the coal mine must 'crawl' to get to the coal face: from this it can be inferred that deep underground there were numerous tunnels instead of actual passages to walk around. Even visiting the space, then, means getting dirty and forcing oneself into a claustrophobic situation. Against this might be compared the almost cavernous workhouse, which is 'inhabited by a population' that range in age from new-born children to old men dying. The space is created as offering no solace for anyone of any age: to be in the workhouse means to face a life of poverty. There is little hope, then, should you end up in either a coal mine or a workhouse.

These spaces are also described as having a religious significance in that they are either like hell or some other place where torture and uncomfortable conditions are common. That the men are 'half-naked' in Source A suggests the heat of the mine. These workers are also 'kneeling' — the conditions in which they work, then, are certainly below any standard that we might expect today. The writer explains how the place is 'like hell', which is then supported through the list, which outlines the 'heat, noise, confusion darkness, foul air' and the 'unbearably cramped space' of the mine. The workhouse environment in Source B, however, is also unforgiving, as evidenced by the story of the young child who dies in the second paragraph. The yard is also described as 'squalid', suggesting how dirty it is. Another room of the building is described as 'a kind of purgatory' — like the mine, this is a transitional space in which people die. Both texts then use references to hell, life and death to suggest the overall poor conditions.

Question Three: Exemplar

You now need to refer only to **Source A** from lines 12 to 27.

How does the writer use language to describe working at the coal face?

[12 marks]

Orwell uses language throughout the extract to emphasise the sense of industry happening at the coal face. That the writer describes the coal face as a 'wall' implies its size, casting it almost as something to be climbed over or knocked down. Verbs such as 'driving' to describe how the workers put their shovels into the ground and 'flinging' to describe how they move the rocks emphasises their strength and the hard work happening below ground. This continues towards the end of the extract when the coal is 'shot into tubs', 'dragged to the cages and hoisted to the outer air' — Orwell's verbs manage to capture the speed with which the coal moves and its weight.

Orwell also balances both metaphorical and literal meanings of phrases to somewhat romanticise the coal. The phrase 'fog of coal dust' implies how thick and impenetrable the air would be below ground. That the 'beam' of a lamp cannot break through the 'fog' furthers this, with the word 'beam' suggesting the power of the lamp. However, the air below ground is so dark that even this 'beam' cannot break through. The idea of a 'fog of coal dust' is thus describing the coal face within terms both literal and metaphorical. This continues later in the extract when the writer describes how the 'glittering river of coal races' down the conveyor belt. The metaphor adds a sense of beauty to the coal, especially the word 'glittering', which juxtaposes the blackness of the coal with ideas of light and worth (this is preceded earlier in the passage when the writer describes the 'shiny black wall' of the coal face). The word 'river' implies these hard lumps are flowing, adding to the sense of movement.

Nonetheless, Orwell does allow negative implications to come into his description. The alliterative 'deafening din' suggests the noise of the belt as the rocks are carried away. Moreover, that the workers are 'feeding' the coal onto the belt suggests the hunger of industry that, presumably, cannot be fulfilled.

Question Four: Exemplar

For this question, you need to refer to the **whole of Source A**, together with the **whole of Source B**.

Compare how the writers convey their feelings about the people they encounter.

In your answer, you could:

- compare their different attitudes
- compare the methods the writers use to convey their different attitudes
- support your response with references to both texts.

[16 marks]

Throughout Source A, Orwell expresses a respect and admiration for the work the miners do in spite of such difficult circumstances. Throughout the third paragraph of the extract Orwell continues to add the numerous challenges the men face in the mine, going into detail about how kneeling 'doubles or trebles the work'. As the paragraph continues, Orwell piles on other complications, such as the 'suffocating' heat and the coal dust 'that stuffs up your throat' – this is an environment that quite literally tries to kill those working within it. Dickens likewise uses listing methods to here suggest the challenges faced by those living in the workhouse. The penultimate and final paragraphs of the extract both begin with 'In another room', accretively adding to the picture of sadness and suffering depicted in the workhouse. Whilst Dickens pities the inhabitants of the workhouse, therefore, Orwell suggests ways in which the mine workers can be admired.

Dickens suggests that there is a 'population' living in the workhouse. To emphasise this Dickens explores various people and describes their bodies. For instance the 'nurse' of the itch ward is described as 'flabby, raw-boned, untidy' with a 'shabby gown' and 'dishevelled head'. However the young girl aged twenty-three on the ward with mad women is noted as being 'very prettily dressed, of most respectable appearance and good manners'. Dickens emphasises how she 'was by no means of the same stuff, or the same breeding, or the same experience, or in the same state of mind' as the other women on the ward. Dickens's repetition of 'same' ironically stresses her difference from the others. Yet the girl is also struggling mentally and is being driven mad by the noises on the ward. Eventually, she will become the 'same' as those other women; Dickens therefore shows the ways in which workhouses affected its inhabitants, even those who did not deserve to be there (the girl has been sent to the workhouse because she suffers from epileptic fits). As part of Orwell's praise of the men in the mine, he compares them through a simile to 'iron-hammered iron statues'. Where Dickens suggests how the workhouses prompt a degeneration in the inhabitants of the workhouse, Orwell does admit to having a 'pang of envy' for the 'toughness' and bodies of the mine workers. In this way, the two writers suggest alternative methods of writing about the poor conditions of the working poor.

Yet Orwell's praise of the worker's bodies is deserved given the environment in which they work. The onomatopoeic 'rattle' of the conveyor belt suggests how annoying that noise might be; Orwell then repeats the word in the same sentence in the simile 'like the rattle of a machine gun'. Not only does the repetition suggest how common the noise is, but Orwell's simile suggests the men in the mine are at war with the environment in which they work. As already suggested, the details about the conditions of the mine support this view. It is unsurprising, then, that Orwell expresses such pride when writing about the workers, for they are cast as heroes (supported also by the statue simile, which suggests their actions should be commemorated). Dickens also uses sound effects in Source B to capture the workhouse setting: the old women are 'chattering and chuckling', with the alliteration and repetition of 'chattering' adding an inverted idea of madness to their expressions. For Dickens, the workhouse truly is a mad place: the juxtaposition in the phrase 'party of pauper nurses' captures how the space is one of confusion and irony. Thus, although both writers explore how individuals face adversity, where Orwell expresses his admiration for the mine workers, Dickens suggests how unpleasant and disturbing Victorian workhouses were.

A now disused coal mine.

Question Five: Exemplar

'Although we look back to the Victorian period and are shocked by how harshly poor people were treated then, we can still see the same issues in society today.'

Write a speech for a school assembly that explores the concept of inequality in today's society.

(24 marks for content and organisation
16 marks for technical accuracy)
[40 marks]

As I've studied English Literature for my GCSE qualification, I've been struck by the many examples of inequality. From the glaring social inequality in An Inspector Calls to the racial inequality in To Kill a Mockingbird, inequality is a theme that can be identified in almost any of the texts studied, from Shakespeare to Austen to Hardy.

Indeed, looking back through history, the most-studied events and time periods are remembered, really, because of inequalities that were present or that were the driving force behind historical events: for example, the social inequalities that were arguably a major factor in the French Revolution; the gender inequality behind the Suffragettes' fight for electoral equality; and the wealth inequalities prevalent in feudal societies. We look back at the past and we see that it was full of inequality, and we may feel that comparatively we now live in an improved, fairer and more equal society.

However the truth is that our society — though having improved in terms of the prevalence of material comforts, the availability of technology and in access to education — is still riddled with the same inequalities faced by other societies through history.

And whether or not you are someone who experiences a great deal of inequality, or who in fact (probably unintentionally and unwittingly) benefits from these inequalities depends pretty much entirely on when, where and to whom you are born. We can, as they say, choose who we become, but really we cannot choose our set of circumstances and which hurdles of inequality we will have to overcome, or be overcome by.

Of course I am not saying that there have not been great wins for equality over the years and that we should not be proud and glad for those. There have been massive positive shifts in equality for people of different races, different genders and those with disabilities. There are more charities and support groups than ever to support people from all walks of life. All this should of course be celebrated.

An early twentieth century photo of a Suffragette out on the streets campaigning.

Nevertheless, it is clear that despite all these positive changes, inequalities in these areas and in others are persistently pervasive. The events of 2020 highlighted many of these: great disparities in medical provision around the world, the deep-rooted racial issues that sparked the Black Rights Movement, the injustice felt by families who had to rely on poorly organised free school meals to be able to feed their children, and the fight to rid the world of a President that embodied the attitudes that allow these inequalities to exist unchallenged.

Inequality is still as intrinsically integrated into our human society as it has been. I believe in fact, that wealth inequality has possibly increased; with such great advances in technology and the ability to get what we want when we want it, some people have sped ahead and built themselves an empire of comfort and commodity, whilst others have been left behind and live their life in ways that the majority of us in this room cannot even fathom. People who see loved ones die unnecessarily, all because they can't see a doctor. People who consider themselves lucky to have a paltry meal each day. People for whom clean water is as precious as their measly yearly earnings.

These inequalities ingrained into our society are so large and such a part of the structure of our human lives that I don't believe that they can ever be eradicated. Having said that, I also believe that could be a great deal lessened if we learned to pull together as human beings across the world, harnessing that spirit of togetherness and empathy that was kindled during the pandemic. We need to learn to work together not just in times of crisis, but in times of stability too, because when things are going well for us, there are undoubtedly many people out there who are still suffering.

Printed in Great Britain
by Amazon